ABOUT HANDICAPS

First published in 1974 by Walker Publishing
Company, Inc. Reprinted 1991.

Published simultaneously in Canada by Thomas
Allen & Son Canada, Limited, Markham, Ontario.

ISBN: 0-8027-7225-0
ISBN: 0-8027-6174-7(HC)

Library of Congress Catalog Card Number: 73-15270

Printed in the United States of America.

10 9 8 7 6

ABOUT HANDICAPS

An Open Family Book For Parents And Children Together

by Sara Bonnett Stein

in cooperation with
Gilbert W. Kliman, M.D.
Director

Doris Ronald
Educational Director,
The Cornerstone Nursery-Kindergarten

Ann S. Kliman
Director,
Situational Crisis Service

Phyllis Schwartz
Community Coordinator

The Center for Preventive
Psychiatry
White Plains, New York

photography by Dick Frank
graphic design, Michel Goldberg

Walker and Company
New York, New York
Created by Media Projects Incorporated

A Note About This Book

When your child was a baby, you took him to the doctor to have him immunized for childhood illnesses. The injections hurt a little, but you knew they would prepare his body to cope with far more serious threats in the future. Yet there are other threats as painful and destructive to a child's growth as physical illness: Separation from his parents, a death in the family, a new baby, fears and fantasies of his own imagining that hurt as much as pain itself. These Open Family Books are to help adults prepare children for common hurts of childhood.

Caring adults try to protect their child from difficult events. But still that child has ears that overhear, eyes that read the faces of adults around him. If people are sad, he knows it. If people are worried, he knows it. If people are angry, he knows that too.

What he doesn't know—if no one tells him—is the whole story. In his attempts to make sense of what is going on around him, he fills in the fragments he has noticed with fantasied explanations of his own which, because he is a child, are often more frightening than the truth.

We protect children because we know them to be different, more easily damaged than ourselves. But the difference we sense is not widely understood. Children are more easily damaged because they cannot make distinctions yet between what is real and what is unreal, what is magic and what is logic. The tiger under a child's bed at night is as real to him as the tiger in the zoo. When he wishes a bad thing, he believes his wish can make the bad thing happen. His fearful imagining about what is going on grips him because he has no way to test the truth of it.

It is the job of parents to support and explain reality, to guide a child toward the truth even if it is painful. The dose may be small, just as a dose of vaccine is adjusted to the smallness of a baby; but even if it is a little at a time, it is only straightforwardness that gives children the internal strength to deal with things not as they imagine them to be, but as they are.

To do that, parents need to understand what sorts of fears, fantasies, misunderstandings are common to early childhood—what they might expect at three years old, or at five, or seven. They need simpler ways to explain the way complicated things are. The adult text of each of these books, in the left hand column, explains extraordinary ways that ordinary children between three and eight years old attempt to make sense of difficult events in their lives. It puts in words uncomplicated ways to say things. It is probably best to read the adult text several times before you read the book to your child, so you will get a comfortable feel for the ideas and so you won't be distracted as you talk together. If your child can read, he may one day be curious to read the adult text. That's all right. What's written there is the same as what you are talking about together. The pictures and the words in large print are to start the talking between you and your child. The stories are intense enough to arouse curiosity and feeling. But they are reasonable, forthright and gentle, so a child can deal with the material at whatever level he is ready for.

The themes in these Open Family Books are common to children's play. That is no accident. Play, joyous but also serious, is the way a child enacts himself a little bit at a time, to get used to events, thoughts and feelings he is confused about. Helping a child keep clear on the difference between what is real and what is fantasy will not restrict a child's creativity in play. It will let him use fantasy more freely because it is less frightening.

In some ways, these books won't work. No matter how a parent explains things, a child will misunderstand some part of the explanation, sometimes right away, sometimes in retrospect, weeks or even months later. Parents really can't help this fact of psychological life. Nothing in human growing works all at once, completely or forever. But parents can keep the channels of communication open so that gradually their growing child can bring his version of the way things are closer to the reality. Each time you read an Open Family Book and talk about it together, your child will take in what at that moment is most useful to him. Another day, another month, years later, other aspects of the book will be useful to him in quite different ways. The book will not have changed; what he needs, what he notices, how he uses it will change.

But that is what these books are for: To open between adult and child the potential for growth that exists in human beings of all ages.

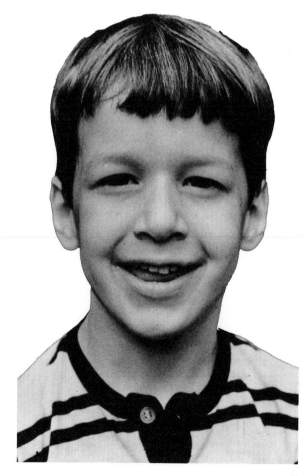

This is Matthew.

And this is Joe.

Joe has cerebral palsy. He is one of the 18 million handicapped people living amongst us in our schools and jobs and neighborhoods right now. In his own community live other handicapped people: A grandmother who is blind, a farmer with one arm amputated, a boy scout deaf in both ears, a retarded baby. And so it is everywhere. Handicaps are not rare.

But they are more frightening. Probably we are scared by notions we hardly know we have —that the deformed are evil, and their deformities contagious. Yet probably each of us has sensed those ideas—in a moment of brushing against a hunchback, or avoiding a blind man. We dare not stare at those people because they seem too awful to look upon. We stifle our curiosity. We hide how we feel, and our fears leak out in discomfort and aversion. We find it all so hard to speak of that it becomes unspeakable.

This book is to give you and your child pictures to stare at, handicapped people to speak about, uncomfortable feelings to share; because that is how people—children and adults—become easier with what is strange to them.

Some people
don't like Joe.
He can't walk right.
He falls down.
That scares Matthew.

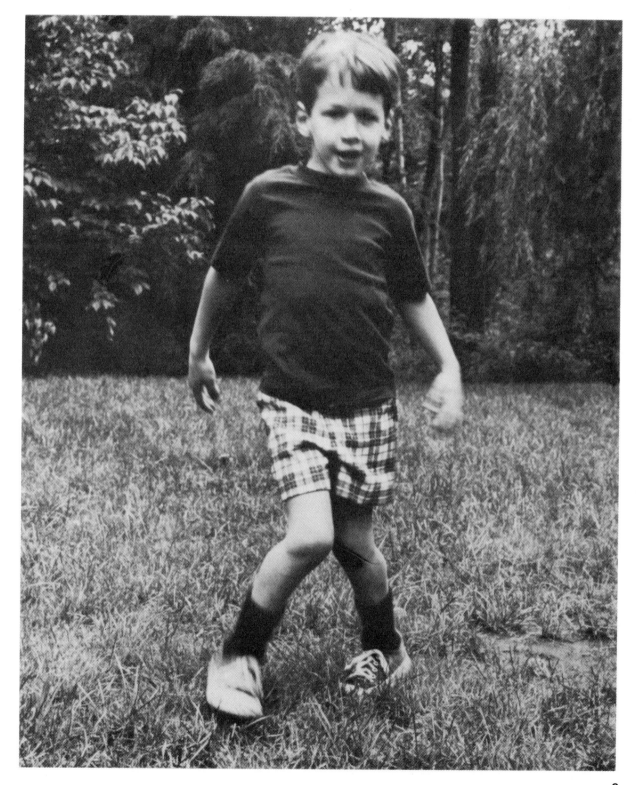

As a child grows from babyhood, he comes to know his own body; he is his face and inside his face; he is his skin that fits him; he is his limbs that do his bidding. And a healthy child feels strong and good and likes himself. But he also learns that knives cut and stones bruise, mosquitoes bite and matches burn. His skin that fits so nice is not strong enough to keep him from harm; in his rush of curiosity his own fingers get pinched, his own feet trip him up. Scraped knees and bumped heads kindle a new uneasiness—that worse things might happen to a child's body. Seeing Joe is proof of what Matthew fears. It can happen: A damaged child. When Matthew imitates the way Joe walks, he is trying to find out what it means, and if this handicap is something he could bear—if it happened to him. It is one way of getting used to Joe.

It can be explained to a child that mimicking hurts another's feelings. But Matthew can practice the strange way Joe walks all he needs to when he is just with his own family. It is no different than playing Pin-The-Tail or Blind Man's Bluff to feel what it is like to be sightless.

Matthew doesn't like Joe's crooked legs. He copies the way Joe walks.

When Matthew jumps and runs so fast he reassures himself another way: His body is super-good—nothing can ever go wrong with it. But he can't convince himself for long. Because something is already wrong—his little toe is crooked.

Most of us can remember back to times when we scrutinized our own bodies with the sharper eyes of childhood—when the conformation of our bellybutton was as mapped as the location of each mole or wart or the pattern of our palms. No doubt each person, searching so diligently for both uniqueness and perfection, has found some small imperfection too. Ears that seem too long, a bulgy navel, a nose tipped in a fashion we wish it weren't.

Matthew's toe is his secret imperfection, raised by his concern to the status of a deformity. It may seem silly from the perspective of our broad grown-up world, but in Matthew's small world his toe is his handicap.

Whenever Joe comes to play, Matthew jumps and runs around very fast. He makes sure his own legs work right. He is afraid they could get like Joe's.

There is already something wrong
with Matthew's little toe.
It sticks up and won't stay down.
He has tried to keep it down
with Band-aids
They don't work.

It's just his little toe,
but he worries about it a lot.
He thinks it could
make him walk funny too.

No one can see the crooked toe inside his leather boots.
It's a secret.

Matthew starts wearing his boots and army hat and his big belt all the time. They make him feel like nothing bad can happen to him because he looks so strong.

The bossy child and the boastful one, the show-off and the fighter, the fancy dresser and the cap gun toter: All these children, like Matthew, puff up their outsides a little to keep their insides safe.

But no buttoned-up shirt, no tucked-into-boots, tight-belted pants, are really going to work. Inside, the little boy with the crooked toe is very scared of the little boy with crooked legs.

Joe wants to wear the hat too. He comes toward Matthew, walking his funny way.

Matthew
pushes him
right down.

No one automatically knows what's going on with children. People have no more than ordinary ways of finding out: Watching, listening, picking up on thoughts, tuning in to feelings, sometimes catching and sometimes missing what is important to their children. Matthew's father doesn't really know what his small son is so upset about. He's never worried about the toe; he likes Joe a lot. Right now, not sure what happened, or why, or how to help, all Matthew's father can do is comfort, and give.

Sometimes the sensitivity of a parent lies in just that kind of caution: Not judging too fast; not condemning a cruel effect before the cause comes clear. Not naming a child mean when he might be scared. Not adding guilt when he might give relief. Waiting—to be sure there is no mix-up between who a child is and what he has done.

As he learns more about what has happened, Matthew's father can make clear to his son that he doesn't want him to hurt another child; that a better way to deal with scary feelings is to talk about them.

Then Daddy sees that something's wrong. He holds him in his lap. Matthew asks for sunglasses. He doesn't want to see Joe's legs so much.

These can be the roots of a child's fear: That damage could happen to him—an accident, sickness. That he might deserve it—a punishment for being bad, for thinking wrong. And that, so visibly punished, a handicapped person must be bad indeed—like what a child knows from tales and television: Scarred monsters, bandaged mummies, shuffling zombies. Having "something wrong" is proof of doing something wrong.

This way of thinking is deep in all of us. Damage as a punishment is expressed in cautionary tales—the troubles of Curious George, the horror of Captain Hook. It is in Grimm and Aesop, in the common phrases of warning with which we raise our children.

To Matthew, this man with a hook is a bad man. He wants to get away.

This is the store that sells sunglasses.

Matthew sees a man going in there. He has a hook where his hand should be.

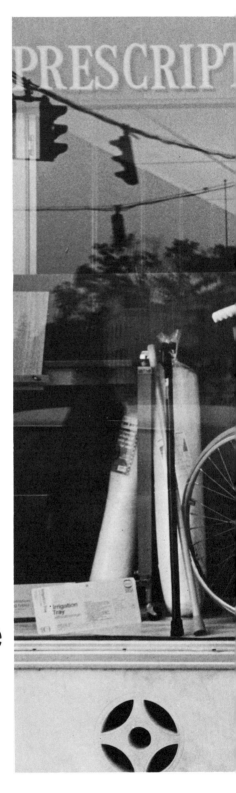

For many people it is uncomfortable to talk with the handicapped. To ask directly what is wrong, and how he got that way, and what life he leads seems impossibly probing and cruel. But never to speak of it is a double-edged sword that hurts both the handicapped and the able-bodied. To the handicapped it means that others find his limitation too distasteful for ordinary conversation; it means isolation and strangeness, shame and sadness. To the able-bodied, it means burying feelings and questions, stuffing them back inside until they press against us, distorting the ease with which we might have come to see and know the person inside the crippled body. And buried feelings leak out in confusing ways: Prejudices we don't understand, irritations and meanness we can't control, nervousness and worry we suspect aren't sensible but cannot stop.

In his son's tense face Matthew's father has guessed the fear that is causing so much trouble. It is time not to get away. It is time to look at these scary things and, by facing them, to grow beyond the bondage of fear.

Matthew tries to pull his daddy outside again.

Handicapped people are only people. Their faces, like our faces, can be read. Their moods, like our moods, show. Their smiles say the same as our smiles. This is an open, friendly man. Matthew's father feels it, knows it. He can ask questions of him and trust answers from him.

Most handicapped people have been handicapped a long time. They are used to it. The cerebral palsied child in this book, his parents, the man with one arm, are ordinary people who want very much to help. They understand our fear because they have felt it themselves. They understand our need to share because they need sharing too. They understand that curiosity is good, and staring goes with learning, and knowledge is necessary. It was Joe's mother who suggested he wear shorts, so other children could really see his legs. It was Mr. Bello who wanted to pull up his sleeve, because he knew children wonder what is under it. Both of them gave us facts that are in this book.

But Daddy walks right up to that man. He says, "Mr. Bello, this is Matthew, and I think he needs to know about your hand."

The man says why he has no arm. It was hit with bullets when he was a soldier in a war long ago. It couldn't work anymore. The nerves and muscles were ruined. He needed an artificial arm instead. Mr. Bello says he was scared when all this happened to him; he was ashamed of having only one arm. He worried that people wouldn't like the way he looked; and that he wouldn't be able to do things anymore.

But he is still himself.

People like him as they always did.

He is used to having one arm,

and he is not scared anymore.

He shows Matthew how the

artificial arm works: It is attached

by a strap around his back

and to his other shoulder.

When he moves his shoulder,

the strap pulls the hook open.

He can pick up money.

And even light a match.

He can take off
the hooked arm
when he goes to bed at night.

What if things don't go so well?
What if in a store, on the street, a
child shrills: "Why is he bent that
way?" "Look, he's got no legs!"
"I don't like ugly people like her."

What if the person is a stranger,
and looks hurt, and isn't friendly?
We want to hush the child up; to
say, "Don't point," "Don't stare;"
to pull away; to simply disappear.
But neither we nor the handicapped will disappear from this
world.

It will not hurt further to quietly
agree with a child's observation:
Yes, something serious must have
happened to that man or that
woman. And it will not hurt further to add that it is something you
can talk about more when you
get home.

Matthew can touch it.

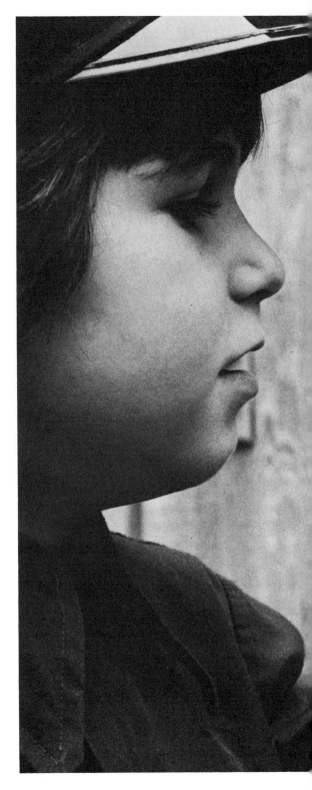

A uniform, a favorite ring, crossed fingers and sunglasses—they are flimsy protections that betray those who hope such magic works. Matthew came to the drugstore to buy sunglasses to protect his seeing, and at that very place was forced to look. He wore boots to guard his toes and feet and legs, and saw a man who lost an arm. He topped himself with an army hat, but that hurt man was a soldier. What protected and defended him is wiped out all at once.

But no one easily or willingly gives up those things that seemed to keep him safe. Matthew may still want long pants, no matter how hot the weather. He may need a Band-aid, no matter how tiny the injury. His growth will be measured, slowly and only a little at a time, in the moment of question, the minutes of a conversation. Now and again, and tomorrow and next week, and other years from now, Matthew's father will agree, "A child could think that; a boy might be afraid of that. I once felt those feelings too." And over and over he will add as simply as he can the facts his son needs to know about his own toe, Joe's legs, Mr. Bello's arm.

For lots of days and lots of weeks, Matthew and his daddy talk about the man with one arm and about Joe's legs. They talk about Matthew's crooked toe too.

These are facts about Joe's legs, in words he can understand: Joe has had cerebral palsy from the time he was born. He can't make his legs straight now. He can't walk any other way yet. It's not a sickness you can catch. A little part of his brain doesn't work right. It is the part that tells his legs how to move. Because his legs don't move right, they also don't grow straight. Every other part of Joe works very well, and always will.

Joe used to have to walk on tip-toe, but he had an operation that made his feet flat to the ground the way they are now. He has to have another operation to make his legs straighter. He does special exercises called physical therapy that are helping him to walk better. It's a lot of work for Joe to do what other people do easily.

These are facts about Matthew's toe: Matthew's toe has always been like that. It will not get worse. It will never make him walk a funny way. It is just the kind of toe he has—like he has a certain kind of nose and hair and eyes and fingernails. It may be different from other toes, but it is fine and likeable like all the rest of him.

Joe comes to play. He is smiling. He is just Joe, Matthew's friend. He can have the sunglasses.

In time, Matthew gets less worried, less ashamed about his toe. Now he can show it to people—if they are friends. Now he can go barefoot—if he is at home. His boots aren't so important to him anymore; he forgets to wear them. He doesn't struggle with Band-aids these days to hold his toe in place; he doesn't care that much. But now the crooked toe has another surprising part to play in Matthew's life: It becomes a bond between two boys. Because Joe is crooked too, he is the first allowed to touch the toe, to try to straighten it, to talk seriously about it, and to joke about it too. Matthew is allowed to touch Joe's legs, to see his scars, to press against his knees and feel the crookedness. And Joe can say that he is crippled.

Matthew can ask about his legs; he tries to straighten them. "You can't," says Joe. "They're crippled."

The two boys share a sense of something suffered in common—one boy a big thing, one boy a small thing—but to each of them, something wrong. As they talk, and as they tease and touch and look, both find a way to take in the realness of being crippled, of knowing for sure the legs cannot get straight, of feeling easier with the way things are, of living with the truth that some things can't be changed. Knowing what can't be done, two boys are free to get on with what can.

And Matthew can show Joe his secret toe. It doesn't seem like so much wrong anymore. It's just the way he is, his own kind of toe.

Matthew and Joe together will build more than buildings. Over years, past these beginnings of courage to ask and touch and know, beyond the ending of this book, two boys will confide fears, share experiences, learn new facts, weigh consequences. They will measure themselves not by army hats or super leaps, not by crooked toes and legs that don't work well, but by their real strengths and limitations. They will dream fewer impossible dreams of what they might do. They will try, and find out. They will not turn from what they fear. They will look and see and test their strength, and find that it is there. And the two boys together will discover what so many people need to know. The handicapped have a gift to give the able-bodied: Proof that people with damaged bodies can live whole inside themselves.

Matthew's feet work very well, and Joe's hands work very well. They decide to build something.

And what they build is really wonderful.